The Art of Taking Action

How to Stop Overthinking, Get Over Your Fears, and Become Insanely Proactive

By Hung Pham
http://www.missionandpossible.com

Your Free Gift

As a way of showing my gratitude, I'm offering a resource that's exclusive only to you.

It's tough not to feel lost in life. The secret is to find out what changes are needed and how to make those changes. In my free eBook, I'll show you how to:

- Remove self-limiting beliefs using this one simple trick
- Stop worrying about the future so that you can focus on the present
- Find the best advice on what to do in your current situation
- Stop living in the past and how to start moving forward
- Appreciate your life more by reframing your thinking
- And much more

>> GO TO http://www.missionandpossible.com to download this free eBook

The Art of Taking Action: How to Stop Overthinking, Get Over Your Fears, and Become Insanely Proactive

Introduction

Do you find yourself living life with regrets wondering what could have been?

Maybe you're well off with a stable job but do you feel like you're slowly wasting your life away?

Do you have a burning passion that you want to pursue but can't out of fear?

Let this book show you how to eliminate the fear and create the life you want to live.

Society says you're supposed to live a certain way; get a well-paying job, buy a nice car, and own a big house.

What they don't tell you is doing all this will cause you to fall into debt. As a result, you slave away at a job you hate and start to wonder if this is the life you really wanted.

I know the feeling; I've been there before.

But one day I read a quote that would change how I thought about life forever.

"Everybody Dies but Not Everybody Lives"

Take a moment and let it sink in. Sure everybody dies but how does everyone not live?

Bronnie Ware, a former nurse who cared for the terminally ill, wrote a very touching article called "The Five Regrets of Dying" after being accustomed to hearing her dying patients reveal their biggest regrets in life.

Here are the five regrets taken directly from the article:

Regret #1: *I wish I'd had the courage to live a life true to myself, not the life others expected of me.*

Regret #2: *I wish I didn't work so hard.*

Regret #3: *I wish I had the courage to express my feelings.*

Regret #4: *I wish I had stayed in touch with my friends.*

Regret #5: *I wish that I had let myself be happier.*

Do any of these regrets resonate with you? Maybe all of them?

After graduating from college in 2004, I struggled with finding my purpose in life. I had a well-paying job but felt lifeless on the inside.

For the next few years, I found myself resenting people who were happier than me and had direction in life.

To simply put it, I was bitter.

My heart was filled with jealousy and envy. How could others be happy while I was miserable?

I was no longer motivated.

But rather than feel sorry for myself and mope around the house, I decided to do something about it. I was tired of being unhappy and resentful. I needed to take action.

I needed to make a change, but not just any change.

I wanted to make one small change first to try and get myself started. I didn't want to aim for a lofty goal and become discouraged if I didn't achieve it.

It was important for me to get started on a good note and that's exactly what I did.

Once I made that change, I continued making another small change and another until it became habitual.

And before I knew it, **my life started to improve immediately as a result of continuously making small changes.**

Within two years of following this system, here were some of the goals that I was able to accomplish:

- I paid off $50,000 worth of debt

- I won a startup competition building a product within 54 hours

- I left my 9 to 5 job to become an entrepreneur and built a six figure business within two years

- I've taught hundreds of entrepreneurs how to make their first dollar

- And most importantly I started to live my life with purpose

None of this would have been possible if I didn't start with making one small change. Any change no matter how big or small is a start and as long as you start, you're on your way.

Why are small changes so powerful?

Take some common questions people have about themselves:

"I hate my job, but how can I find something better?"

"I know what I need to do, but why am I so afraid to do it?"

"Why does it always seem like other people get breaks instead of me?"

"I deserve more in life, but how do I ask for more?"

No matter how insurmountable you think your problems are, to overcome them, all you need to do is start.

Remember, Rome wasn't built in a day.

This is why small changes are necessary. Trying to tackle a large problem can seem impossible. Instead, break it down into smaller and smaller chunks until it becomes manageable.

Doing this will create the motivation you need to propel you forward. Will there be bumps along the way? Of course, but that's with all things in life. If it were easy, it wouldn't be worth it.

The small changes in this book are broken down into three sections that are meant to improve your life and maximize your ability to take action:

1. Small Changes That Create a Fearless Mentality

2. Small Changes to Take Action and Be a Leader

3. Small Changes to Create a Life of Purpose

Create the foundation of success for yourself with one small change today

Every small change presented in this book is a change that I have made for myself. It's tested and proven.

It's a change I know that works and I encourage you to try each one. They are not difficult to do; you just need to keep practicing until you've mastered it.

For the best results, read this book once and then go back and select the small changes you want to start with. Make a list and make it a goal to finish each and every one.

The tips in this book are going to be short but right to the point. They're going to be awesome nuggets of information that will help you get started right away.

I can promise you that once you're done, the quality of your life will improve dramatically and you will begin to live with purpose and fulfillment.

Here's to taking action and seizing the life you want to live!

Small Changes That Create a Fearless Mentality

I hate fear. I hate the feeling of having my stomach tied in a knot, but I know that living a life with purpose begins with creating a fearless mentality.

That is why I have chosen this to be the first section of this book. When you're creating a fearless mentality, you set the foundation for other small changes.

What does it mean to be fearless?

Let's look at some of the most successful people in history such as Michael Jordan, Steve Jobs, and Oprah Winfrey.

14

Guess what these three celebrities had in common aside from being rich and influential?

They all failed early on in life and despite their failures, went on to become extremely successful.

It's because they were fearless and relentless in their pursuit of success.

Michael Jordan, the greatest basketball player in history, didn't make his high school basketball team as a sophomore.

Oprah Winfrey, one of the richest and most powerful women in the world, was fired from her job as local TV news anchor in Baltimore.

Steve Jobs, one of the greatest entrepreneurs ever lived, was fired from Apple; the company he started in his 20's.

These are all billionaires who at one point or another suffered dramatic setbacks.

Imagine being Steve Jobs and getting fired publicly from the company that you started in a garage. Can you imagine how much public humiliation he endured as a result of this?

Now Steve could've crawled under a rock and disappeared from the face of the Earth, and nobody would've blamed him. But he didn't, he went out and started other companies, one of which happened to be Pixar.

It's not easy to come back from setbacks, but Steve was able to do it.

Apple floundered in the years following Steve's firing, but he was eventually brought back to save the company from the brink of death

It's safe to say that without Steve Jobs, there would be no Apple. Steve was fearless.

I want you to be fearless too.

It all starts with building a fearless mentality that produces winning results. Winning is 95% mental and 5% everything else. That's why I've chosen these 13 effective small changes to help you create a fearless mentality.

#1. Visualize Success

I was born with a vivid imagination. As a child, I would play with my Transformers for hours by myself because I used my imagination to create an entire story line.

As an adult, I don't use my imagination as much as I'd like to anymore. However, when I do, I visualize what I want for myself and the positive effects are amazing.

One of the best ways to create a fearless mentality is to visualize success. It's is a popular technique that is practiced by many successful athletes all over the world.

When athletes talk about taking the game winning shot all their life as a child, they are referring to visualization. They are visualizing their success.

What does success mean to you?

Does it mean finally having the courage to ask your boss for the promotion you deserve?

Does it mean finishing the full marathon race that you've been training months for?

For some people, success could be something big as climbing Mount Everest or something as small as losing 10 pounds.

Whatever the challenge is, you can use visualization as a technique to face it head on.

Here's how I recommend visualizing success:

First find a place where you can be alone with your thoughts and away from distractions.

Some of my favorites are:

- Going for an outdoor run in the morning

- Taking a hike away from the city

- Working out at the gym

- Taking a long scenic drive somewhere

- Alone at home with scented candles lit

Next turn your phone off or put it on mute. It's important that your phone doesn't distract or disturb you. Don't worry; you can survive for 15 minutes without your phone.

I want you to begin visualizing what success means to you.

Visualizing doesn't mean you have to close your eyes. It just means you have to create an image in your mind of what success is. You can close your eyes if you like, just make sure you're not doing it while driving.

Once you have that image in your mind, I want you to zoom in on it. Don't worry about anything else and just focus at this point. Now do the following:

1. Picture the challenge you are struggling with.

2. What does it look like?

3. What does it feel like?

4. Identify the goal you want to achieve based on your challenge.

5. Picture the solution. See yourself accomplishing the goal. What are the steps you need to take to make it happen?

6. What does it look like?

7. What does it feel like?

8. Use any or all of your five senses to help you with visualizing.

9. Once you see that vision of success, I want you to embrace the moment and make a mental imprint.

10. Store it somewhere in your memory so that you can refer to it again and again.

For example, here's how I would visualize myself finding a better job.

Picturing the Challenge

I hate my job; I feel like I'm only there because I need a steady paycheck. I want something better, but I'm not sure where to start. I've been applying to jobs online but haven't gotten any replies in months.

I'm frustrated. Am I not good enough? What am I doing wrong?

Identifying the Goal to Achieve

What do I need to do differently? I need to find a way to stand out. Applying online just puts me in a pile with thousands of other applicants.

I know that internal referrals hold more weight than simply applying online. How can I get an internal referral?

Picturing the Solution

I need to meet people at the companies I want to work at and find a way to have them refer me. Let me brainstorm a few ways I can achieve this.

- *I can ask my current network for introductions*
- *I can reach out to people through LinkedIn and ask them to lunch or coffee so that I can pick their brains*
- *I can go to professional networking events and meet people in person*

Picturing Success

Through the various methods I came up with, I was able to meet and build relationships with people who work at companies I want to work for.

One of the people I met happened to refer me to a position in her group that just opened up. She thought I would be a great fit for it.

I interviewed and got the job. Not only did I find something better and aligns with my interest, but I also got a huge pay increase.

Once you have the image of success, follow the steps in your visualization to make it happen.

When visualizing, try to focus on the feelings you feel; the sense of purpose and accomplishment. Do you feel free? Do you see yourself as a happier person? Does it make you eager to accomplish this goal?

Sometimes visualizing can be a 15-minute activity or an hour long; it's entirely up to you. You'll notice that the more you visualize yourself achieving a goal; you'll start taking action to do it.

#2. Reach for The Stars, Land on the Moon

In life, I've met people who set extremely high goals, and I've met those who don't bother to set goals at all. Guess which type ends up happier in the long run?

Hopefully, you said the ones who set extremely high goals.

When I speak with people who don't set goals for themselves, I always ask them why that is. One of their reasons is that they don't want to disappoint themselves if they can't reach their goals.

That's understandable, but it's also counterproductive.

Let's say you want to work for Google or Facebook, but you're afraid of applying because it's super competitive. You're worried that if you do get an interview, you might bomb it. On the one hand, yes you'd be avoiding failure, but at the same time, you'll never get the opportunity to work there.

What's costlier in the long run?

I'm a big believer in setting goals, in fact, the higher and more descriptive the goal the better. Why? Because goals help you set direction in life. When you have direction, then you know where you're going.

Which goal sounds better to you?

Goal 1: Lose 2 - 5 pounds in two months

Goal 2: Lose 10 pounds in 6 weeks with 10% body fat on a strict low carb diet, working out twice a day.

Now Goal 1 sounds pretty easy, just lose somewhere between 2 - 5 pounds in two months. You can probably get away with just starving yourself or taking diet pills to reach that goal. But what have you really accomplished by doing so?

Starving yourself is unhealthy, and nobody knows what the long term effect of taking diet pills are. These aren't good ways to go about accomplishing this goal.

Goal 2, on the other hand, seems harder and more intense. Here you are aiming to lose more weight in less time and doing so with 10% body fat using a combination of healthy dieting and working out.

Now, which goal would you choose? Personally, I'd choose goal 2. Goal 2 is definitely the harder of the two to achieve, but you should always choose the harder path.

Let's say instead of losing 10 pounds in 6 weeks with 10% body fat you ended up losing 8 pounds in 6 weeks with 12% body fat. You didn't achieve your goal but guess what; it's still good. You went about it the right way.

In fact, it's probably better than most people.

When you set extremely high goals and fall slightly short, you're still much farther ahead than others who set easy goals or don't set them at all. How you achieve your goals is just as important as the goals you achieve.

Remember, when you reach for the stars, you'll always land on the moon.

#3. Begin with The End in Mind

Since we're on the topic of setting goals, another reason why people don't like to set goals is that they don't know where to start. I see this a lot with people who are overwhelmed with their problems.

To solve a particular problem, begin with the end in mind.

In other words, start with the goal and then work backward on how to achieve it.

Let's say you have $20,000 worth of credit card debt. Trying to figure out how to pay it all at once can be downright scary. Some people become paralyzed with fear and choose to just ignore the problem.

But this is not the solution; not even close. If you want to get out of credit card debt, you've got to take action.

Here's how you can approach this goal by beginning with the end in mind.

Let's say you want to pay this debt off in a year. Let's break it down by months:

$20,000 / 12 months = $1667 (the amount you would need to pay per month to reach this goal.)

If $1667 per month is too much for you, then try 18 months (1.5 years) or 24 months (2 years).

Using 18 months we get:

$20,000 / 18 months = $1111

Using 24 months we get:

$20,000 / 24 months = $834

Does paying $834 a month for 24 months sound more affordable to you?

It may take a little longer, but at least you have a baseline on where to start. Now that you know you need to set aside $834 every month, you can create a spending budget that works.

You took something that seemed insurmountable, and by using simple math, you broke it down into manageable tasks. That's the beauty of beginning with the end in mind.

You can use this small change for any goal you want to achieve. Let's try this with another example. Let's say you want to save $50,000 to make a down payment on a house. Right now you only have $10,000 in the bank.

Assuming you want to buy a house in two years, we get the following calculation:

$50,000 - $10,000 = $40,000 you need to save

$40,000/24 months = $1667 that you need to save each month

Now that you have a number, your job is almost done. All you need to do now is to figure out how to save an extra $1667 each month for the next two years.

How would you be able to do this? Here are a few suggestions:

- Eat out less and cook at home more often.
- See if there are things around the house you can sell on eBay.
- Call up your insurance company and see if you can get a lower rate.
- Call up your credit card company and ask for a lower interest rate.
- Cancel your cable TV service and subscribe to Netflix instead.
- Pick up a few weekend and/or part-time gigs on Craigslist.
- Become a driver for Uber or Lyft.

The possibilities are endless. Once you have a number, it becomes basic math. Beginning with the end in mind helps you reach your goals by breaking them down into smaller chunks making them less scary.

#4. Give, Give, Give, Then Ask

This is one of my favorite small changes because it's a powerful method for building strong relationships. The foundation for this small change is simple; offer to help others and do not expect anything in return.

Relationships are vital to success because they provide you with opportunities for advancement and a network for support and advice.

Too often I come across people who only care about helping themselves. They have with a *"what's in it for me attitude.*" Both ways of thinking are extremely flawed.

Instead, offer to help others for a change. If you know someone that can use your help, don't ask, and just help that person. Figure out how you can be of value and do it.

Why is this small change so effective? For several reasons:

- It helps you build rapport if you're meeting someone for the first time and don't have an established relationship. People are usually guarded when they meet someone for the first time. Doing this will help lower their guard.

- It's a very generous gesture, and people will come to trust and respect you because of this. This is the opposite of the *"what's in it for me attitude."* Instead, it's the *"what can I help you with attitude."*

- If and when you finally need a favor, you can ask the people you have helped. Not everyone will replay the favor, but most people will be glad to help you because of all the good will you've built.

Help can come in many forms. It could be something simple as short chat to listen to someone's problems or an offer to take a friend to lunch when they're having a rough day.

Now there's always a risk that you could go out of your way for someone and that person could turn out to be an absolute jerk. It has happened to me before, but it's no different than falling in love.

When we fall in love, we know there's a chance that we could have our heart broken, but that's the risk we take. Eventually, we recover and open ourselves to love again.

If you live your life in fear of falling in love, you rob yourself of one of life's greatest emotions. The same goes for helping others. In the long run, the more people you help will return the favor over those who don't.

If you sense that someone can use your help, don't be afraid to offer.

#5. Start Today

This small change sounds very simple, yet it is one of the hardest to do. That's because it requires you to remove all doubt and jump in head first.

Now think back to the last time you jumped into something head first.

What was it?

Were you jumping into the deep end of the pool?

Maybe you were jumping into a new relationship?

Or perhaps you quit your job to start your own business.

What did you feel? Was it scary? Of course.

Was there an initial shock? You know it.

But regardless of what it was that you jumped head first into, you still made it out okay. Otherwise, you wouldn't be here reading this book right now.

Too often, I'll come across people who have grand visions for what they want to do in life. They talk about the impact they want to make and how they are going to change the world.

However, when I asked them what they're doing to make it a reality, here's what I usually hear:

"I'm not ready yet, I need to keep planning."

"One day I'll get to it. Just not today."

"It's not time yet, but hopefully soon."

"I'm too busy. As soon as I find some time, I'll get to it."

If these sound like excuses to you, it's because they are. Here's a bit of truth for you. You don't need to plan or make time to chase your dreams. I understand the need for planning and can respect those who take the time to plan.

But there's something called analysis paralysis that occurs if you're constantly planning and not taking enough action. You can never plan for perfection, so you'll have to eventually draw a line in the sand and just go for it.

You can and should start today.

If you want to start eating healthier, start today.

If you want to re-invent yourself, start today.

If you want to change careers, start today.

Whatever you want to do, you should start today. It makes no sense to wait until the New Year to make resolutions. If your dreams are important to you then take action and start today.

Remember, done is better than perfect.

#6. Remove Your Negative Core Beliefs

Core beliefs are what we think of ourselves to be true. Negative core beliefs are the negative things that we believe to be true. They can come in many categories but some of the more common ones are:

- I'm a failure
- I can't seem to do anything right
- I'm ugly
- I'm worthless
- I'm needy and weak
- I'm boring
- Nobody will ever love me
- Why would anyone want to be with me?
- I always seem to mess things up
- I'll never amount to anything

Here's a little secret I learned about negative core beliefs; it's all in your head. Whatever you feel or think about yourself, I can promise you that others don't feel the same way about you.

Your family, your friends, your peers; they don't see you the way you see yourself.

I'll touch on a couple of actionable tips in this chapter on removing your negative core beliefs, but if you want an in-depth system, I highly recommend reading my other book.

Negative core beliefs are damaging because they create a mental prison that prevents you from taking action to improve your life. You're already defeated before you even start.

In order to remove the negative core beliefs, we must change them into positive core beliefs. Here's how you do that:

Stop Reinforcing Your Negative Core Beliefs

Whatever negative core beliefs you feel about yourself, STOP right now. The longer you allow yourself to believe these thoughts, the harder it is to remove them. The first step is to stop reinforcing them.

Challenge Your Negative Core Beliefs

Another way to change your negative core beliefs is to challenge them. If you're a failure, look at everything you've accomplished so far. Do you still feel like a failure?

If you feel boring or worthless, ask your closest friends what they think your best qualities are. Then see if what they say reminds you of a boring or worthless person.

Whatever it is that you doubt about yourself, challenge it by asking others if it's true.

Create Change in Your External World

One of the best ways to change a negative core belief is to actually make a change in your life. If you think you're boring, then go and do something that isn't boring. Join an activities group, plan an event, do anything that isn't considered boring.

Nothing solves a problem faster than taking action. Don't dwell on the things that make you frustrated, do something about it.

Use Affirmations

Using affirmations is one of the best ways to restructure and reposition a negative core belief. If you feel like a failure, ask yourself why you feel that way? Is it because you didn't land the high profile job you spent three months interviewing for?

Now restructure and reposition your thought process. Instead of feeling like a failure, think about how awesome you were to get so far in the interview process. Out of hundreds of applicants, it came down to you and another person. That itself is an accomplishment.

#7. Look for Small Wins

To leave the comfort of your bubble and take risks requires a high level of risk tolerance. It's not for everyone, but at the same time, we need to take risks to build the life we want to live. When you do decide to take that leap you're going to find yourself facing tough challenges every day.

In order to deal with the roller coaster of emotions, it's imperative that you look for small wins. Small wins can come in various forms. It could be something as simple as a thank you email from a close friend or an accomplishment such as

making your first sale as an
entrepreneur.

Small wins are important because when
times are tough, and you feel like
quitting, they serve as small bursts of
energy to help get you going. Small wins
are like affirmations because they
provide positive reinforcement.

When you're trying to find out who you
are and what you want to do in life,
you're going to be faced with a lot of
questions such as:

"Am I doing the right thing?"

"Did I make the right decision?"

"Am I really cut out for this?"

And what these small wins do is they
serve as reminders why you must
continue to push forward. They serve as
validation that you're on the right track.
So how do you find and celebrate small
wins? Well, imagine you have a baby. If
you're already a parent, then this
example will be easy to understand.

As a parent, every milestone in your baby's development is a considered a small win. The first time your baby speakers. The first time your baby walks. The first time your toddler learns how to use the toilet.

Now to other people, these milestones might not mean as much as they do to you and that's okay. You are the parent and should be celebrating these accomplishments because they are achievements that make being a parent worth it.

Now take the same approach to whatever it is you are taking that risk to do. If you are packing up and moving to another country, look for small wins to celebrate. If you just quit your job to start your own business, look for small wins to be proud of.

In tough times, small wins are proof that you are living the life you were born to live.

#8. Always Choose the Harder Path

Nobody likes things that are hard. As a child I would eat mac and cheese everyday over broccoli if I could. But there's a reason why mac and cheese is unhealthy for you and broccoli isn't.

Tough managers, projects that drive you nuts; these things are hard for a reason. But in my experience if there's something that I'm confident about; it's to always choose the harder path.

Why the harder path?

Because all the things you want in life are outside your comfort zone.

Because if it were easy, then everybody would be doing it.

Because nothing ventured is nothing gained.

Because in the end, you come out a better person regardless of the outcome.

If an opportunity that presents itself to you doesn't make you nervous, then it's not worth your time. Every opportunity in my career that has scared me to death has always been worth the risk.

If you're disappointed with how your life has turned out, take a look at all the decisions you've made until this point. It's possible all the choices you've made so far haven't worked out for you. If so, then it's time for a change.

Instead, start by doing the opposite of what you've been accustomed to. Start doing things that make you feel uncomfortable such as:

Example #1

Let's say you're out on a Friday night and you see a cute guy/girl at the bar. Instead of coming up with a million reasons why he or she may not be interested in you, go and talk to the person. Don't worry about being rejected, just focus on the conversation and leave it at that.

Example #2

If there's an opportunity for you to lead a big project work, take initiative and go for it. You might be worried that you're not qualified for the job but you miss 100% of the shots you don't take. If you know it's a good step for your career, go for it.

Example #3

Did you get into a fight with your spouse or someone close you to recently? Reach out to the other person and apologize. Take responsibility for your actions regardless of who you think is wrong or right. It's hard to swallow your pride, but at the end of the day do you want to be happy or right?

These are just a few examples, but hopefully you get what I'm trying to show you. When in doubt always choose the harder path; the one that you don't want to take.

In fact, if you just focus on always taking the harder path, I promise that you will surprise yourself and those around you with how much you can accomplish.

Take the path of most resistance.

Small Changes to Take Action and Be a Leader

The first group of small changes in this book taught you how to eliminate fear by creating a fearless mentality. This next group of small changes is all about taking action.

When you start to take action, people will begin to notice the new you. And if you continue to take action people will see and identify you as a leader. A leader isn't someone who sits back and tells others what to do; that's called a manager.

A leader leads by example

A leader is the first to show up and the last to go home.

A leader inspires others to take action.

A leader leads by elevating those around him/her

A leader serves others.

Those are traits of a great leader.

I understand it can be scary at first. How do you lead and inspire others if you've never been a leader before? What about the pressure of letting people down?

You may think you're not capable of being a leader, but I'm here to tell you you're wrong.

Anyone can become a leader. The challenge is whether you choose to take action to become one or not. Fortunately for you, I've identified seven small changes to help you create a leadership mindset and leadership qualities.

Are you ready to be a leader?

#9. Find Your Tribe

If you've ever watched National Geographic, Animal Planet, or the Discovery Channel, you'll notice that animals tend to live in groups. Some animals like elephants and zebras live in small groups while ants and bees live in large colonies.

They do this for several reasons, but the main ones are:

- **Protection** – weak animals like fish swim in schools to protect themselves by having more eyes watching out for predators.

- **Hunting** – animals like wolves and hyenas hunt in packs to improve their chances of catching and killing prey

- **Raise Their Young** – animals like monkeys live in groups where there are few parents and many young. By living in groups, the parents can pool together resources.

- **Building Shelter** – terminates are great examples of animals who work together to build shelter for their large colonies.

As humans, we are no different. We can accomplish more together than we do alone. That is why we seek companionship.

Are you surrounded by people whom you have very little or nothing in common with? Maybe you're itching to connect with people who inspire and motivate you.

To be a leader you must first seek other leaders. This is also known as finding your own tribe. Merriam-Webster dictionary defines a tribe as:

A group of people that includes many families and relatives who have the same language, customs, and beliefs.

I like to think of a tribe as like-minded people with common beliefs, goals, and interests. Basically, you're trying to find where you belong.

Why are tribes important?

Think of a tribe as a community but smaller. A tribe serves as your support system when times get tough. Your tribe can consist of your family, friends, peers, and colleagues; anyone who aligns with your goals and beliefs.

A tribe can help you with career and life advice; they can make the necessary introductions to help you get ahead. Your tribe can simply be an ear to hear you out. Whatever the problem, your tribe understands because they've been there before.

So what if your family, friends, or peers aren't like-minded as you? How do you find your tribe then?

Here are a few of my favorite methods:

1. Join a <u>Meet Up</u> group. You'll be surprised at how many various groups there are on Meet Up. If you have a particular interest, chances are other people do as well.

2. <u>Linkedin</u> is especially great if you have a particular person you'd like to connect with. It's also great if you are trying to change careers and need advice. There's a function on LinkedIn called InMail that you get when you use a paid account. InMail allows you to message anyone without having to be connected to that person.

3. Volunteering is one of the oldest and easiest ways to find your

tribe. It can also open many doors to great career opportunities. When I wanted to learn more about startups, I volunteered at startup events. This gave me great exposure, and I met some really awesome people who ended up being friends and mentors.

4. Ask your current network. There's a high chance that someone knows someone that knows someone who may be just like you.

5. There are social and mobile apps out there now that will help you connect with people. It's amazing to see how far technology has come these days.

#10. Be Present and Make Yourself Known

When I first graduated college, I worked as an engineer at a Fortune 100 company. I worked really hard and did whatever was asked of me, but what I noticed was that my peers would get recognition on projects before I would.

This led to them being promoted and me being frustrated.

I didn't think they worked harder than me; if anything we all worked equally hard. But for some reason, I wasn't being recognized. I decided to sit back and observed what was going on.

Here's what I discovered.

- They were always the first to introduce themselves to new people
- They were always the first to start conversations
- They were always dropping into people's cube to say hi and make small talk

In short, they were always making themselves known.

What I had been doing was the complete opposite. I kept my head down. I was focused on my work and hoped that my work ethic would speak for itself. I wasn't making myself present in the minds of others.

So I begin to mimic my peers. I asked people how their weekend was every Monday. I would try to crack jokes and make people laugh before every meeting started. If I needed something work related from a coworker, I would make small talk first before diving into work conversation. I wanted people to learn more about me and vice versa.

And sure enough, things began changed. I started to get more recognition for my work. It wasn't because I was worker harder but because I was making myself present and known.

The good news is that it doesn't take much effort to make yourself present and known. Even if you're an introvert, these tips will work for you. Here's what I recommend:

- Be the first to introduce yourself when you meet someone for the first time.

- Always be the first to greet people when you see them. Make eye contact and smile.

- If you're on a conference call, be the first to speak. If you want to provide feedback, be the first to speak instead of letting someone ask for your opinion.

- If you're in a conversation and you see people who aren't actively participating, extend an invitation. Ask them for their valued opinion. Make the other person feel valued.

These are just a few tips out of many, but it's enough to give you a good start on how to make yourself present and be known.

#11. Take Charge When Possible

In order to take action and live a life of purpose, you have to find opportunities where you can take charge. Taking charge doesn't necessarily mean leading an army into battle but rather taking initiative when possible.

If you're not used to taking charge or if you're shy, start small. Taking charge can come in many forms such as:

- Planning a birthday party
- Planning a small get together amongst friends
- Organizing an activity at work
- Planning a road trip

- Organizing a reunion

You may come to find that you're already doing these activities. If so, then great because you're demonstrating leadership qualities. People already see you as a person of action. Now take that mentality and apply it to other aspects of your life.

If there's a problem at work that you think could be fixed or improved, go for it. You don't need to ask for permission. Just raise the issue to your team and let them know you are going to take on the challenge.

If you think your team will benefit greatly from a team outing, organize one. If it turns out well, then organize a few others and keep it consistent. Your peers will tell others at work and you'll be known as the fun person that brings people together.

In your circle of friends, see if there are opportunities to lead. If they are talking about planning a trip somewhere, make it happen. Organize a road trip or vacation, become a leader amongst your friends.

Being a leader can also stem from negative situations. If you're encountering problems in your family don't sit back and wait for others to fix the issue. Take initiative to try and make things better. Be the one that people can turn to during tough times. They will remember you.

#12. Getting Over the Fear of Rejection

Let's face it rejection sucks. Not getting into the college you wanted, or the promotion you worked so hard for, or the woman of your dreams can hurt. There's nothing pleasant about rejection.

Yet rejection is a part of life we must all learn to live with.

We've all experienced some form of rejection before. It's very likely we will experience rejection many times before we die. However, the sooner we get over our fear of rejection, the sooner we can begin to build a life with purpose.

But how do we get over the fear of rejection?

Being rejected is a huge blow to the ego because it's the part we hold near and dear to our self-esteem. When our ego is hurt, it affects how we feel about ourselves. However, with a few simple tricks, you can quickly learn to get over your fear of rejection.

1. **Don't take it so personally:** If you didn't get a job you really wanted, it doesn't necessarily mean you weren't good enough. It's possible that you just had a bad day interviewing. There will be other opportunities.

2. **Ask a stranger to borrow a dollar:** There's no quicker way to get over your fear of rejection than to put yourself out there. Next time you're out, ask a stranger to borrow a dollar and see what happens. You may not get a dollar

but how did rejection feel? Not that bad right?

3. **Look at the bigger picture:** I was once fired from my job at a huge tech company. At first I was furious because it was unexpected. Once I calmed down and looked at the bigger picture, they actually did me a favor. I hated my job, I wasn't motivated, and being fired actually led me to bigger and better things.

4. **Use the fear of rejection as the ultimate motivator:** Fear can do one of two things to you. It can cripple you to the point where you can't function or it can be the ultimate motivator to push you beyond your wildest dreams. It all comes down to how you accept and deal with the fear of rejection.

5. **It is a numbers game:** Many men fear approaching attractive women because they don't want to get rejected. My advice is to not put so much emphasis into

any one rejection. Dating is a numbers game, and as long as you keep trying, you're bound to have success.

Like anything we're not comfortable with, it takes time and practice to get used to rejection. However, once you get used to it you'll look at it as something as normal as breathing.

#13. Practice Makes Perfect

It's possible to take action with the small changes above and not see the results you are expecting. It doesn't mean you're not leadership material; you just need to find the right context to demonstrate your leadership abilities.

I always challenge myself to keep trying new things. I do it because I love to learn and when I find something I'm passionate about, my leadership ability naturally comes out.

And as you try out new things, involve others by asking for feedback. Don't be the guy that nobody wants to work with because you're cocky. Be open and transparent, ask for feedback, and offer to help.

Once you find the right context to bring your leadership qualities out, keep practicing until you've mastered it. In the popular book "Outliers: The Story of Success" by Malcolm Gladwell, he repeatedly mentions a concept known as the 10,000 Hour Rule.

If you've never heard of it or haven't read the book, the 10,000 Hour Rule simply states that the key to success in any field is to consistently practice a specific task for a total of around 10,000 hours to completely master it.

Well what does 10,000 hours come out to in years?

Let's say you want to become a master at boxing. If you practice boxing for 3 hours a day, 6 days a week, it will take you approximately 11 years to master boxing. The math breaks down like this:

3 hours a day x 6 days a week = 18 hours practiced a week

10,000 hours to master / 18 hours practiced a week = 556 weeks

556 weeks to master / 52 weeks in a year = 10.5 or 11 years to master

The math shown here is just an example. Of course, the more time you put into practicing, the fewer years it takes to master. The inverse is also true. The less time you put into practicing, the more years it takes to master.

Here's how it looks if we compare the different scenarios. Assuming you practice boxing 6 days a week, you get the following:

# of Hours a Day	# of Days a Week	# of Years to Master
2	6	16
3	6	11
4	6	8

It'll take time before you find something you are passionate about but once you find it, keep practicing. Master it, and people will look to you as a leader and expert in that field.

#14. Develop Your Emotional Intelligence

Being a leader is as much about understanding people as it is about leading them.   However, if you're not able to control your emotions, it is unlikely that you'll able to understand others.

You must first develop an awareness of your emotions and make smart decisions on how to effectively use them in any given situation. Being able to manage your emotions affects whether others perceive you in a positive or negative light.

Imagine losing your cool in a situation that doesn't warrant it. How would others look at you? Maybe a little hot headed? Maybe a bit out of control? Either way, it's not a favorable look.

I once lost it while I was driving with my little two nieces in the back seat. Some jerk cut me off, and I cursed loudly. I did it because I was angry, especially since I had young children in the car.

I didn't engage in road rage, but because I cursed in front of my nieces, I wasn't proud of myself. With kids, you have to be careful with what you say because their soak up everything they see and hear.

I wanted to set a good example for them, but I failed. I shouldn't have let my emotions get the better of me, but I did. They always saw me as the fun-loving uncle, but on that day for a moment, they saw an angry side of me.

But let's say in a tense situation you keep your cool and make smart decisions. What happens then?

For one, people see you as cool, calm, and collected. They see you as someone who doesn't get rattled; someone that can stay focused and makes sound decisions even in the tensest moments.

More importantly, they see you as someone they can rely on. This is extremely important because it builds trust.

They see you as a leader.

Take the time to be in touch with your emotions. Try to develop a deeper understanding of your own values and motives, your strengths and weaknesses. Some people call this being sensitive, but I like to think of it as having emotional intelligence.

It's a type of self-awareness.

When you are self-aware, you're able to cut through the noise and hear what's really being said. You're not listening through the filter of others. This is a very critical skill of being an effective leader.

Once you're able to develop a high level of emotional intelligence, use it to try and create win-win results out of tough situations. Create solutions that others can participate in and embrace. Be open and flexible to feedback and different perspectives.

Leadership through emotional intelligence is about building teams and empowering others to act in the best interest of everyone. Create an environment of openness and collaboration and let your leadership abilities naturally flow forward.

You can rule with fear, or you can rule with love.

Which do you choose?

#15. Know Your Strengths and Weaknesses

A big part of taking action is knowing what your strengths and weaknesses are. This way when you do take action, you put yourself in a position to succeed when you give yourself the opportunity to use your strengths.

You may have an idea of what your strengths are, but I highly recommend checking out Gallups Strengths Finder. If you have some time, read Strengths Finder and take the assessment. You'll get a report of what your top 5 strengths are along with an action-planning guide.

In my opinion, Strengths Finder does two things really well.

First, they validate things you may already know about yourself. For example, it may say you are a great connector. You might have suspected this already if you're a friendly and outgoing person.

Second, they provide in-depth suggestions for how to use your strengths to maximize your potential.

Why is it important to know your strengths and weaknesses?

Well if your strengths happen to be teamwork and loyalty, then you know you will most likely thrive in a team environment collaborating with other people.

On the other hand, if your strength is being a creative out of the box thinker, you may want to avoid an environment that relies heavily on processes and structure to get things done.

The same can be said of knowing what your weaknesses are. Knowing what you're not good at or what you don't like will help you avoid situations that are less favorable to you.

In addition to that, knowing your weaknesses allows you to find others who are strong in that particular area to collaborate with.

The old conventional way of thinking was to work on your weaknesses so that you are well rounded. I'm not a big fan of that perspective. Instead, I prefer to find out what I'm really good at and double down on those areas.

Then I can surround myself with others whose strengths are my weaknesses.

You see this often with startup co-founders; one person is more technical, and the other person is more business oriented. This creates the foundation for a successful partnership.

I like to use my strengths and weaknesses as a way to expand my social network. You don't necessarily have to go into business with the other person. It's just good to have people with different strengths that you can turn to for advice if needed.

Even if you already have a good idea of what your strengths are, I highly recommend taking the Strengths Finder assessment to learn how to maximize your strengths.

#16. Become an Excellent Communicator

Whenever I find myself stuck or feeling uninspired, one of my favorite activities is to go to YouTube and search for motivational speech videos. These usually include:

- College graduation commencement speeches
- Football locker room pre-game speeches
- Inspiring interviews or talks
- Inspiring stories of people overcoming challenges

What I enjoy most about these videos is not so much the topic but rather how it's being told. Being an excellent communicator is about being a master storyteller. How does your message get through to your audience?

Can you connect with people and influence them?

The ability to share your vision with others, the ability to gain support and cooperation; these are all traits of an excellent communicator.
Communicating is just as much about listening as it is about speaking.

When you start by listening to others first, then they are more likely to listen to you.

So how do you become an excellent communicator?

First start by being an excellent listener. When you understand another person's goals and objectives, you can clearly articulate how their aspirations can be aligned with your vision.

I always like to start with a simple question such as, *"How are you doing or How are things going?"*

From there, depending on the response, I'll usually follow up with another question like, *"How can I help you with _____?"* where the blank is something that person is struggling with.

For example, let's say I'm having a conversation with my friend Patrick over a drink.

> **Me:** *"Hey how's it going?"*
>
> **Patrick:** *"It's been okay, the wife and kids are good, but work is another story."*
>
> **Me:** *"Oh why is that?"*
>
> **Patrick:** *"They're overworking and underpaying me. I think I need to find something better soon or else I'll go crazy."*

Me: *"Yea, I hear you on that one. So how can I help you with your job search?"*

That's it. It's not rocket science. It's simply giving the other person your full attention and space for them to open up.

Nothing ruins relationships faster than having an inflated ego. Rather than being prideful and arrogant, take the opportunity to understand the other person's perspective. This will give you a level of authenticity and transparency that people will respect.

Also, make sure to follow up on whatever action comes from offering to help. This ensures that you are a person of your word. And don't make any promises you can't keep.

Just like with the 10,000-hour rule, being an excellent communicator takes a lot of practice. Whether you're talking to a friend, a stranger, or in a public setting, always look for opportunities to practice listening and speaking. Eventually, you will come to master this important skill.

Small Changes to Create a Life of Purpose

When I was young, my parents wanted me to become a doctor. Coming from a traditional Asian household, it was the prestigious career to have. As a child, they tried their best to drill it into my head.

They went as far as sending me to a national youth leadership convention on medicine in high school to further my education. When I came home from the 10-day trip, I told them I didn't want to be a doctor anymore.

In college I studied computer science because this was during the first boom of the dot com era and technology was all the rage. After graduation, I spent one year working as a web engineer only to realize I sucked at writing code.

Most of us don't have the slightest clue when it comes to what we want to do with our lives. I thought I knew what I wanted to do when I was in school, but I was wrong. I thought I knew what I wanted when I graduated and got a job, but I was wrong again.

I didn't figure it out until my early thirties, and when I did, the lifestyle I was living didn't reflect the person I wanted to be. I knew that I needed to make small changes.

When I sat down to write this book, my goal was to share with you what has worked for me over the years to help me get over my fears and find my way. Now that you've taken action to make significant changes to your life, it's time to work on maintaining it.

If you're not sure that you're living a life of purpose, here are some questions to help you figure it out:

- If you look back 20-30 years from today will you have any regrets on things you didn't do?

- If financial stability weren't an issue, would you still continue to do what you do today?

- Are you doing everything you possibly can to make yourself happy?

If you're not able to answer these questions with definitive answers, then it's likely you're not living a life of purpose.

This last group of small changes will work on creating a lifestyle of purpose. Some of these changes will force you to step back and reflect on your current lifestyle while others are very small incremental changes that you can do right away.

#17. Reassess and Simplify Your Life

One of the first steps to creating a life of purpose is to step back and reassess the needs in your life. When I first did this exercise, one of the first needs to go were material items; specifically, any large purchases that were holding me back.

I'll be honest for a minute. It's nice to drive a fancy new car. But you know what's not nice? Being in debt. While it would be nice to buy a brand new car, I didn't really need it because doing so would've put me in debt.

And as long as I was in debt, I couldn't be free to do the things I wanted to do in life.

Next to go was any monthly expenditure that I absolutely didn't need to have. To figure this out, I started by tracking my spending on a daily basis for a few months. I categorized all of my spending so that I could easily spot unnecessary items to cut out. As much as I love In-n-Out burger, I knew it wasn't a necessity.

I rarely watch TV yet I was paying for cable. It turns out services like Netflix and Hulu make for suitable and cheaper replacements. The best part was staying home to watch a movie instead of going to the theaters.

I had to think about what was a need versus a nice to have in my life. I want you to do the same. The goal here is to simplify.

If there's stuff around the house you don't need anymore, don't throw it away yet. See if it has any value first. Any material item with value that I didn't need anymore, I sold it on eBay or Craigslist.

To me, I considered that making investment money for my future business idea. Anything I couldn't sell, I donated to charity because I didn't need the clutter in my life.

When I finally simplified my life, I felt liberated and free. The less stuff I had meant the less energy and time needed for maintenance. We live in an age of so much consumption that sometimes you forget how little you need to live a meaningful life.

I'll end this chapter with a quote from one of my favorite movies of all time, Fight Club,

"The things you own end up owning you."

#18. Find an Accountability Partner

To ensure that you continually make small changes to eliminate fear and live a life with purpose, you need an accountability partner. An accountability partner is someone who makes sure you stay accountable for the things you commit to doing.

Now most people think, *"I don't need an accountability partner, I'm already responsible."* but let me share the following story with you. In my 20's I bought a gym membership because I wanted to get fit.

For the first two months, I went to the gym by myself 3-4 times a week. I was eager to go and work on my beach body but, after two months, I began to slack off.

Now I only went to the gym 1-2 times a week and made all sorts of excuses like:

"I had a long day at work today."

"I just ate, I'm too full to work out."

"It's raining outside; I'm lazy to go."

Around this time, a good buddy of mine also signed up for a gym membership at my gym. He was new to working out and didn't want to go alone. I offered to go with him so he wouldn't be by himself.

Now I found myself going to the gym 5-6 times a week. When I was tired from a long day at work, I stilled forced myself to go. When the weather was ugly outside, I dragged myself to the gym.

I did this because my friend depended on me. If I didn't go to the gym with him, I knew that he wouldn't go. We became accountability partners to each other. As a result, we got our beach bodies much faster together than we would've alone.

That's the magic of having an accountability partner.

What makes a great accountability partner? Usually, I look for someone with the following characteristics:

- **Trustworthy:** It's important to find someone you can trust to keep you accountable. You should also be able to trust his person to keep things confidential if needed.

- **Open and Honest:** If you're falling behind on your goals, your partner has to be honest enough to call you out and give you constructive feedback. They only want the best for you.

- **Challenging:** Find a partner that will challenge you to accomplish your goals. Rather than judge, they help by pushing you.

- **Responsible:** You need a partner that is dependable enough to stay on top of you and check in regularly to track your progress.

- **Mature:** There are going to be times when things are tough and you feel like giving up. Your partner should be mature enough to give you the tough love you need to power through.

Who can be an accountability partner? A family member, a close friend, a colleague, your spouse, basically anyone you trust with the characteristics listed above.

If you can't find an accountability partner, I recommend blogging about your goals. Sometimes talking on a public platform such as a blog helps create a sense of accountability.

Another option is to participate in public forums that align with your goals and who you are as a person. Often in these forums, you will find like-minded people that will help you push towards your goals.

These options won't replace an accountability partner, but they make for suitable replacements if you can't find one. However, I would still recommend trying to find an accountability partner first.

#19. Create a List of 3 Things to Accomplish Each Day

As I got older, I found it harder to keep track of everything I needed to do. To fix this, I began creating to-do lists. I hated doing this at first because every time I created one, it had a billion things on it.

Okay maybe not a billion but there was always a bunch of things on my lists that I needed to do. It got to the point where whenever I looked at my list, I got overwhelmed and ignored my list.

Eventually not much got done.

To make things more efficient, I modified my to-do list by only listing three things I wanted to accomplish each day. It's that simple. In the morning when I wake up, I think of the three most important things I need to get done that day and write them down on my list.

I find the best time to do this is in the shower.

Now if there was something that took more than a day to finish, I broke it down into smaller tasks. This made it easier to work on each day until I completed all the tasks.

For example, if I wanted to create a blog I might not be able to do it in a day. But by breaking it down into smaller tasks, I can work each day until the blog is finished.

It might look something like this:

Day 1:
1. Pick domain name and register
2. Sign up for web hosting service

3. Install Wordpress for my blog

Day 2:
    1. Research and buy a design theme for Wordpress
    2. Install the theme on my blog
    3. Launch my blog

Day 3:
    1. Research what articles to write about
    2. Write and publish first blog post
    3. Share through social media

And if I couldn't get all three things done that day, I simply rolled it over to the next day to finish.

It's very important to keep this list short hence only choosing three things. You want to make it so that it is manageable to do in a day. Remember the importance of small wins that we highlighted at the beginning of the book? Getting things done in a day is the equivalent of achieving small wins.

The other important factor is to put a time block on yourself to get these all done in a day. You'll be surprised at just how effective time blocks are. Without it, you're more likely to push things off as you get distracted or don't feel a sense of urgency.

You can pick major items or minor items to add to your list; it's up to you. Just be sure to pick three things you can accomplish in a day and do it every day so that it becomes routine. When you make this a part of your daily habit, you'll wonder why you didn't start sooner to begin with.

#20. Create a Daily Routine: Wake Up and Exercise!

In addition to creating a list of three things to accomplish each day, let's work on creating a daily routine for yourself. The goal of creating a daily routine is to promote progress and maintain consistency.

For the days that are especially tough and daunting, having a daily routine helps you get through the day because there's not much thinking on your part. You have a routine, and your job is to do it each day until it becomes automatic.

There are two things that I highly recommend as part of your daily routine; the first is getting up early and the second is starting your day with some physical or aerobic exercise.

I was never a morning person in my early twenties. I suspect it was probably due to the late nights studying in college. After I graduated, I still preferred to stay up late into the morning hours. I did this because I thought I could get more done.

As a result, I always had a hard time waking up the next day. I didn't feel normal until lunchtime because I would be so groggy in the morning. Then I noticed that it was affecting my performance at work. I was making mistakes I normally don't make.

I decided to change my routine and started waking up earlier. Instead of 8:30 am I forced myself to get up at 7:30 am. To make sure I started my day off on the right foot, I ran for at least 20 minutes each morning.

By waking up earlier, I created time to get some exercise in. I used to exercise at night, but once I started exercising in the morning, I found that it to be more effective at setting the tone for the rest of my day.

Here's what I liked most about exercising in the morning:

- Exercising in the morning helped me feel energized, and I was able to carry that feeling throughout the rest of the day

- I usually woke up groggy so exercising in the morning helped me "wake up" faster. After 20 minutes of running, I felt sharp and alert.

- After a while, I actually looked forward to waking up and exercising because I was addicted to how good it made me feel.

- Research shows that exercising makes you smarter because you get a good flow of oxygen to the brain. Who doesn't want to wake up smarter every day?

- Now that exercising is a part of my daily routine doing it in the morning ensures that I don't miss it.

It will take some time for you to come up with the best daily routine for yourself, but whatever it is, make sure to wake up early and exercise. Even if you think you don't have time, try to squeeze in 15 minutes of high-intensity cardio exercise.

You'll thank me for this!

#21. Surround Yourself with Positivity and Inspiration

Your environment plays a major role in how you live your life. This isn't just about the people in your life; it's also about your surroundings. Growing up I would come home from college to find my parents fighting over money.

At first, I tried my best to ignore it and focus on school, but over time it became too much to handle. It created such a negative energy throughout the house that it started to take a toll on me. My grades were slipping, I didn't eat or sleep well, and I started to get sick a lot.

It wasn't until I moved out that I finally felt better. That's when I realized how much of a role the environment I lived in affected my life. To help you create a life of purpose, I highly recommend that you surround yourself with lots of positivity and inspiration.

Here are some tips on how to do that:

- I'm a big fan of motivational quotes. Find some of your favorite quotes and either print them out or write them down. Then hang them on your wall where you'll most likely see it every day.

- If you have any role models or heroes, do the same for them as well. Print out their picture and put them up on your wall.

- A lot of times I find that people are too hard on themselves and don't give themselves enough credit. Write down three things you are most proud of about yourself and hang them up.

- Whenever you have the time, listen to uplifting music or motivational audio books. I find this works best when I go for runs or work out at the gym.

This is the most important tip when it comes to surrounding yourself with positivity.

You are who you choose to associate yourself with.

Nothing drags you down faster than those who have no morals, poor character, or are just plain negative. I call these types of people energy vampires because being around them constantly will suck all the energy out of you.

Now I understand that some of these people may be childhood friends and you feel a sense of loyalty to them but the bottom line is this:

The choices they make and how they live their lives will influence the choices you make and how you live your life. You need to be aware of this and be accountable for who you are.

Now this doesn't mean you need to disown your friends, but at least be selective about when and where you choose to hang out with them. Be smart with the decisions you make when you're with them. If something doesn't feel right, then trust your instinct and leave.

On the flip side, similar to Small Change #9 Finding Your Tribe, surround yourself with people who you look up to. They don't necessarily have to be like-minded, they just need to be people who are positive influences in your life and support you in everything you do.

You'll come to see that the more positive influences that you have in your life, the higher your quality of life will be.

#22. Turn Your Passion into a Side Project

What I'm about to say may sound cliché, but it's also very true; if you find something you love to do, you'll never have to work another day in your life. The problem for most of us is how do you find something you love to do and get paid while doing it.

Jack Ma, the founder of Alibaba, said it best when he said:

"A good job isn't something you go out and find. It's something you discover while you're working."

Let's say that you love cooking and taking pictures of the food you make. One of your dreams is to start a food blog. Now it wouldn't make sense to quit your day job because you wouldn't be able to support yourself financially. That would be a risky proposition.

But it's still possible to make this happen while working a full-time job. It requires hard work, dedication, and a lot of patience.

You do this by turning your passion into a side project or side hustle.

I've had the luxury of meeting entrepreneurs who now support themselves doing what they love to do. I met a lawyer who quit his law career to write dating books. I've met people who travel the world ten months out of a year because they live off of their online businesses.

And it was all possible because by turning their passion into a side project.

Now that I've got your attention let's talk about how to get started.

If there are topics that you are passionate about, start blogging about it. I've met entrepreneurs who now support themselves and their families by blogging, and it all started as a hobby. The key to making a blog successful comes down to producing good content and creating value for your audience.

If your passion is a service, focus on being an expert and find clients to sell your services to. Services like web design or being a personal trainer are two easy examples that come to mind.

Try to find two to three clients in the beginning and make it a priority to build good relationships and provide great work. Happy clients always make good references and provide referrals.

In the end, whatever your passion is, make it a priority to do high-level quality work. If you can concentrate on that, the money will follow and once you have enough money you can quit your day job

and make your passion your full-time
job.

This won't happen overnight, but as long
as you're putting time and effort into it,
something good will come out of it.

.

#23. Stop to Reflect Every Now and Then

As I get older, there's one common theme that comes up a lot, and that is:

"Life is tough."

I know it sounds cliché, but it's true. Life only gets tougher as we get older regardless of social class or wealth. There are some things that no matter what we try to do, we can't change.

I'm talking about things like our health, youth, and death which are all interconnected.   While we are young, we are at our healthiest. However, as we age, our health slowly deteriorates.

Of course, there are things we can do like exercise and eat better to be healthier, but it doesn't stop the aging process, it just slows it down. Eventually, we all leave this Earth.

I know it sounds somber, but it's important that you remember this key item. Every now and then, stop to reflect on life. Reflect on who you are, what you've accomplished, and where you want to go next.

Life is busy, and as we get older, it gets busier. We get married and have kids. We pay our bills and save for our children's college tuitions. And somewhere in between, we try to find time to relax only to realize we can't because something else needs our attention.

But I encourage you to take a breather even if it's ten minutes and reflect on your life. Reflect on your day, reflect on your week. Give yourself the awareness to see the path you're on and determine if you need to make any changes.

People who have purpose in their lives, reflect every often. I do this several times a week; so much that it has become second nature. When I reflect, I'm looking at everything I've done up to that point and compare it with the life I want to live.

I'm looking to see if the two are aligned with each other. If they are, I make sure to continue to do what I'm doing. If not, I try to see what areas are out of sync and work on bringing them back in sync.

It's the equivalent of looking in the mirror and asking yourself if you're happy with the person looking back at you. I know you're busy but give yourself the opportunity to reflect every now and then.

#24. Never Stop Learning

I am saving the best for last, as this is my favorite small change of all. Are you ready for it?

Never stop learning.

The only way you'll truly eliminate fear and live a life of purpose is to continually challenge yourself to get better and better every day.

Life never stops teaching so then why do most people stop learning?

Most people assume that learning only happens when they're in school and that's wrong. Most people assume that learning is only necessary when it's related to their job and that's also wrong.

The famous painter Michaelangelo once said at the age of 87, *"I am still learning."* That's the beauty of learning. Learning happens regardless of how old you are.

Now I need you to make me a promise okay?

Promise me that you'll always find time to learn. You can choose whatever it is you want to learn, a new programming language, how to cook French cuisine, or how to create the perfect flower arrangement.

Whatever it is you choose, make sure you set aside time each day, each week to do it. As long as you are learning, you're making progress and giving your life purpose.

Challenge yourself by reading one new book every month and then set aside time each night to read until you finish. Challenge yourself by taking an online class to learn a new skill and set aside time each day to do it.

Complacency is the enemy of progress. Don't allow yourself to be comfortable. Even if you think you have everything you could want, continue to push yourself to be better, to do more, to create a meaningful life.

I will end this final small change with a quote from Henry Ford that I hold near and dear to my heart.

"Anyone who stops learning is old, whether at two or eighty. Anyone who keeps learning stays young. The greatest thing in life is to keep your mind young."

Never stop learning.

Conclusion

Congratulations on finishing this book! Hopefully, at this point, you understand the importance of small changes and what it takes to eliminate fear and live a life of purpose.

Just remember that change doesn't happen overnight, especially if you're looking for big dramatic changes. Instead, focus on small changes that you can easily incorporate into your lifestyle and do over time.

By making them habitual, these small changes will become more and more effective. Pretty soon you won't even notice the changes because they will become second nature to you.

It's not going to be easy, and there will be many days when you feel like giving up. But when those days come, just pull out this book and start reading it again. Remember why you bought this book, to begin with and motivational force that drives you.

It's never too late to create the life you want to live. All you need is the courage to start and the will power to continue improving every day. These 23 small changes are what have worked for me, and my hope is that they will work for you as well.

I wish you the best and good luck on your journey.

Sincerely,

Hung Pham

If you enjoyed this book and want more tips and strategies on building a better life, sign up for my newsletter at: http://www.missionandpossible.com

P.S. If you found this book valuable, could you please take a minute and leave a review for this book on Amazon? Your feedback will help me continue to write Kindle books that produce positive results in your life.

P.S.S. If you enjoyed this book, I highly recommend you check out my other Amazon bestseller books on personal development.

Cheat Sheet

Small Change #1 Visualize Success: create in your mind the image of the life you want to live and the person you want to be.

Small Change #2 Reach for The Stars, Land On The Moon: Set high goals for yourself, even if you don't reach them you'll finish way ahead of others.

Small Change #3 Begin with The End In Mind: Take any goal and work backward by breaking it down into small tasks you can accomplish.

Small Change #4 Give, Give, Give, Then Ask: Always start with the mentality of how you can help others. When it is your turn to ask for help, they will be glad to help you.

Small Change #5 Start Today: Don't put off until tomorrow what you can do today.

Small Change #6 Remove Your Negative Core Beliefs: Whatever negative feelings or thoughts of yourself you believe to be true are not. Turn them into positive core beliefs, so you can move forward.

Small Change #7 Look for Small Wins: Slow and steady wins the race. Look for small wins to get you through tough times.

Small Change #8 Always Choose the Harder Path: All the things you want in life are outside of your comfort zone. When in doubt, choose the harder path.

Small Change #9 Find Your Tribe: Seek others whose goals and beliefs align with yours as they will inspire and motivate you to succeed.

Small Change #10 Be Present and Make Yourself Known: Make yourself known in the presence of others by being the first to take action.

Small Change #11 Take Charge When Possible: Always look for opportunities to exert your leadership abilities.

Small Change #12 Getting Over the Fear of Rejection: Don't let your fear of rejection cripple you; use it as a force to motivate you.

Small Change #13 Practice Makes Perfect: Find the right context to showcase your leadership abilities and keep working at it until you become an expert.

Small Change #14 Develop Your Emotional Intelligence: Being a leader is as much about understanding people as it is about leading them.

Small Change #15 Know Your Strengths and Weaknesses: Put yourself in a position to succeed by giving yourself the opportunity to use your strengths.

Small Change #16 Become an Excellent Communicator: The ability to share your vision with others and gain their support and cooperation are traits of an excellent communicator.

Small Change #17 Reassess and Simplify Your Life: Think about what you need to have vs. what you like to have. The less burden you carry means the more freedom you have.

Small Change #18 Find an Accountability Partner: Find someone you can trust to keep you accountable for your actions and goals.

Small Change #19 Create a List of 3 Things to Accomplish Each Day: Write down three things you aim to accomplish each morning and get it done that day.

Small Change #20 Create a Daily Routine: Create a daily routine for yourself to create constant progress. I recommend waking up early and adding 20 minutes of high-intensity exercise.

Small Change #21 Surround Yourself with Positivity and Inspiration: Create an environment that promotes positivity and elevates you to a higher level. You are who you choose to surround yourself with.

Small Change #22 Turn Your Passion into a Side Project: Take your passion and start bringing it to life by making it a side project.

Small Change #23 Stop to Reflect Every Now and Then: Life is busy but give yourself the opportunity to reflect on the life you're living and the life you want to life. If the two are not aligned, bring them back in sync.

Small Change #24 Never Stop Learning: Complacency is the enemy of progress. Always challenge yourself by learning something new.

About The Author

Hung Pham is the founder of <u>Culture Summit</u>, a conference that helps companies succeed through building strong cultures. Before Culture Summit,

Hung spent over ten years working at several Fortune 100 companies.

In his 20s, Hung dealt with a serious gambling addiction that led to severe depression and financial debt. Through hard work and persistence, he has turned his life around and become a successful entrepreneur. You can learn how too by downloading his free 33-page eBook at www.missionandpossible.com